Especially for:

Mary Jones —
  a gifted teacher!

With love & thanks!
        Amy

Love Is the Best Teacher

Love Is the Best Teacher

Written and Illustrated by

joan walsh anglund

**Andrews McMeel
Publishing**

Kansas City

ISBN: 0-7407-4158-6

Library of Congress Control Number: 2003111242

04 05 06 07 08 KFO 10 9 8 7 6 5 4 3 2 1

Book composition by Kelly & Company, Lee's Summit, Missouri

ATTENTION: SCHOOLS AND BUSINESSES

Andrews McMeel books are available at quantity discounts with bulk purchase for educational, business, or sales promotional use. For information, please write to: Special Sales Department, Andrews McMeel Publishing, 4520 Main Street, Kansas City, Missouri 64111.

For my granddaughter Emily
with all my love

The future begins

in the mind

of a child.

Love

is always

the best teacher.

Every living thing
   responds
      to love.
   The secret of teaching
      is to care
         about your students.
   They will feel it
      and
         they will
                  learn!

A good teacher

changes the world

one student

at a time.

Teach a child
and you touch
the future.

When love

       and wisdom

       go hand in hand,

          a young mind

              learns.

Education
   is not a narrow thing
      of books and rules
but, rather,
      a grand adventure
         of joy and discovery.

Obedience

is not the goal

of education . . .

freedom

is!

If you would teach,

be slow to judge

and quick to praise.

What activity
is happier
or more satisfying
than teaching
a child?

A good teacher

    leaves her mark upon

        our lives

    and, as we move forward

        into adulthood,

    we carry with us, always,

        the imprint of her caring.

She who teaches

also

learns!

Learning

begins anew

with

every dawn!

We teach

with our

every action.

A closed mind

       is a locked door.

It's a teacher's job

       to find its key.

The smart teacher
teaches the mind;
the wise teacher
teaches the heart.

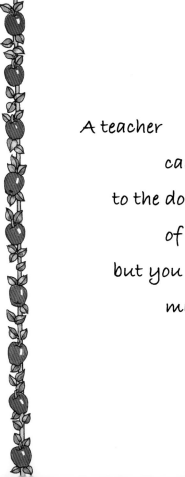

A teacher

        can lead you

    to the door

        of wisdom,

but you

      must

        step through.

A good teacher

helps us

find out

who we are

and points the way

to what we can

become.

The art of teaching

is

the ability

to inspire.

Teacher,

if you have helped

one student

to discover

his full potential,

you have accomplished

your task

here.

Every experience
teaches
and,
used rightly,
strengthens!

A teacher

    lights the candle

        of knowledge

    so a child

        may better

    find his way

        through the mysteries

            of life.

Not every teacher
will inspire us,
but during our
school years
there will be
one
or two,
and that
will be
enough.

Curiosity

is the teacher's

greatest ally.

Once a child's

curiosity is awakened

the teacher's job

is half done!

Learning

makes glad

the mind.

Once we experience

the joy of learning

our lives are altered

forever.

The time to learn

is always

now!

One kind act
         teaches more
than many
         harsh words.

To teach children

one must first

respect them.

Teaching requires

the wisdom

of a sage,

the patience

of a saint,

the caring

of a friend,

and the endurance

of a long-distance runner.

Life is a schoolroom

and love

is the primary lesson.

A teacher

    looks into the minds

        and hearts

      of her students

and calls forth from them

        their very best.

Talent may be given,

but an education

is earned.

For nine months of the year,
a teacher
is the guardian
of a child's mind
and the caretaker
of his future.

The purpose
    of education
  is to light the lamp
    of understanding
within
  the darkness
    that is ignorance.

The positive effects
of a teacher's
good influence
upon us
extend
throughout
a lifetime!

It is a teacher's happiness
to see a young mind
reaching for a star . . .
and,
sometimes,
"catching" it!

To educate

      a child

   may be

      life's hardest

         task

   and greatest

         joy.

It is love,

not reason,

that opens

the door

to the heart.

The highest form

of teaching

is gentleness.

Hold fast to your dreams!

They are the stars

you will follow

to find your way

to the future.

As sunshine

to the flower

is a teacher's

praise

to a child.

Each of our lives

has been made better

because

a teacher

believed

in us.